KB207766

e future

Smart
LISTENING

1.1

Contents

New Friends

A Listen and repeat. 01))

1 Hello **Alex**	2 Hello **Kate**	3 Hello **Ben**
4 Hello **Amy**	5 Hello **Sam**	6 Hello **Ella**

B Listen and number. 02))

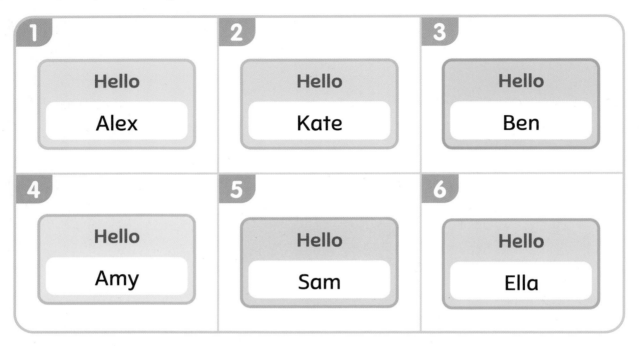

☐ 1 ☐ ☐ ☐ ☐

Sam Ella Alex Amy Ben Kate

Hello. I'm Ella.

I'm = I am

C Listen and check. 03))

1.

Ella   Amy

✓

2.

Alex   Sam

3.

Kate   Ella

4.

Sam   Ben

D Listen and match. 04))

1. ?
Hello
Ella

2. ?
Hello
Alex

3. ?
Hello
Ben

What's your name?
My name's Ben.
What's = What is | name's = name is

A Listen and number. 05))

B Listen and circle. Then write. 06))

1.
Hello	Hello
Amy	Ella

What's your name?

My name's _____Ella_____.

2.
Hello	Hello
Ben	Alex

What's your name?

My name's _____.

C Listen and draw lines. 07))

• What are the kids' names?

Alex   Sam

Kate   Ella   Amy

 Turn! • Listen and answer. 08))

7

My School Things

A Listen and repeat. 09))

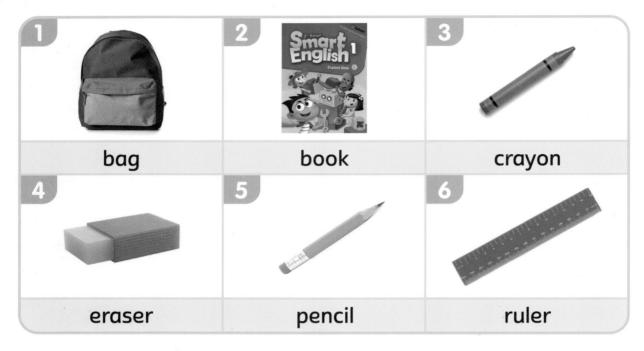

1	2	3
bag	book	crayon
4	5	6
eraser	pencil	ruler

B Listen and number. 10))

This is a book.

C Listen and check. 11))

1.

2.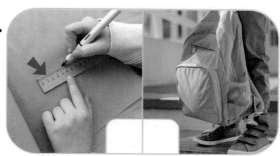

3.

4.

D Listen and number. Then draw. 12))

What's this?
It's a crayon.
What's = What is | It's = It is

A Listen and number. 13))

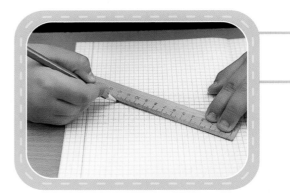

What's this? It's my ruler.

What's = What is | It's = It is

B Listen and circle. Then write. 14))

1.

What's this?

It's a _____.

2.

What's this?

It's my _____.

C Listen and draw lines. 15))

• What is in Amy's bag?

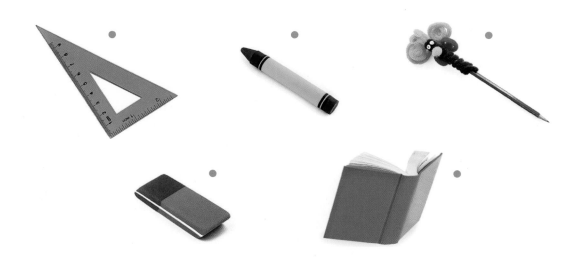

 Your Turn! • Listen and answer. 16))

3 In the Classroom

A Listen and repeat. 17))

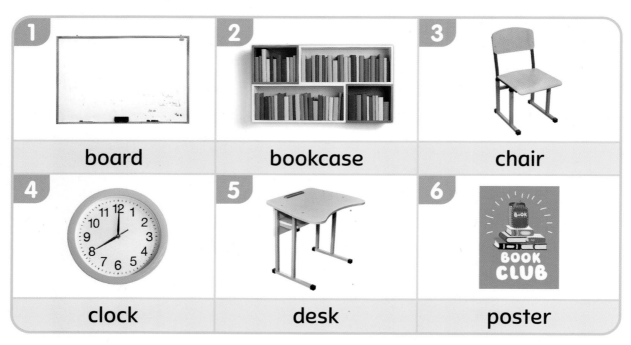

1 board	2 bookcase	3 chair
4 clock	5 desk	6 poster

B Listen and number. 18))

It's a poster.

It's = It is

C Listen and check. 19))

1.

2.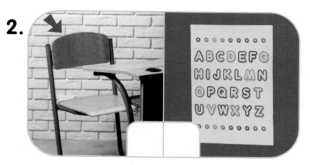

3.

4.

D Listen and match. 20))

1.

2.

3.

What is it?
It's a desk.
It's = It is

A Listen and number. 21))

B Listen and circle. Then write. 22))

1.

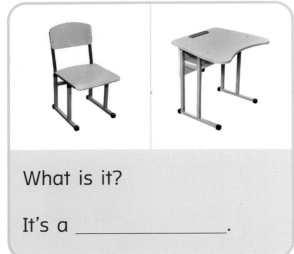

What is it?

It's a _____.

2.

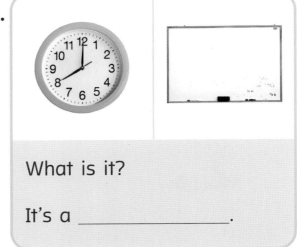

What is it?

It's a _____.

C Listen and circle. 23))

1. What is in the box?

(a)    (b)   (c)

2. Which is Ella's bag?

(a)    (b)    (c)

 • Listen and answer. 24))

A Listen and draw lines. 25))

Sam

Ella

Alex

Kate

B Listen and write. 26))

1. What is the boy's name?

Ken

2. What is the girl's name?

C Listen and check. 27))

1. Who is the boy talking to?

Ms. Kate

A ☐

Ms. Ella

B ☐

2. Which is the boy's desk?

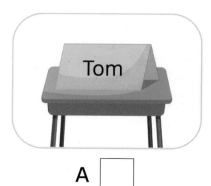

Tom

A ☐

Ted

B ☐

My Family

A Listen and repeat. 28))

1 mom	2 dad	3 brother
4 sister	5 grandpa	6 grandma

B Listen and number. 29))

me

He's my dad.

He's = He is

18

C **Listen and check.** 30)))

1.

2.

3.

4.

D **Listen and match.** 31)))

1. • •

2. • •

3. • •

Who's she?
She's my mom.
Who's = Who is | She's = She is

A Listen and number. 32))

B Listen and circle. Then write. 33))

1.

Who's she?

She's my _____.

2.

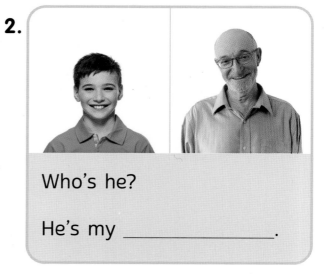

Who's he?

He's my _____.

C Listen and circle. 34))

1. Who is in the album?

ⓐ  ⓑ  ⓒ

2. Who is Ella's friend?

ⓐ
Hello
Tom

ⓑ
Hello
Tony

ⓒ
Hello
Tim

 • Listen and answer. 35))

A Listen and repeat. 36)))

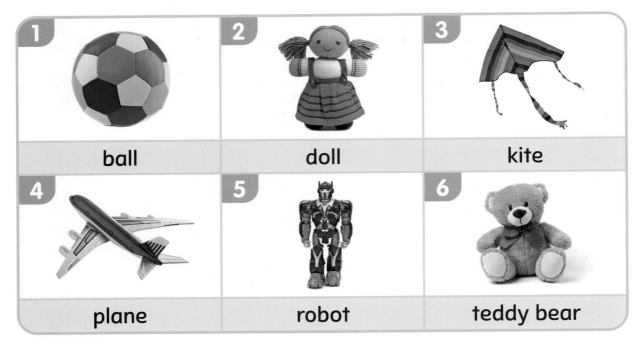

1 ball	2 doll	3 kite
4 plane	5 robot	6 teddy bear

B Listen and number. 37)))

It's a robot.

It's = It is

C Listen and check. 38))

1.

2.

3.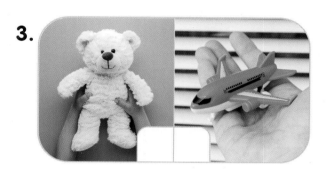

4.

D Listen and number. Then draw. 39))

Is it a ball?
Yes, it is. / No, it isn't.
isn't = is not

A Listen and number. 40))

B Listen and circle. Then write. 41))

1.

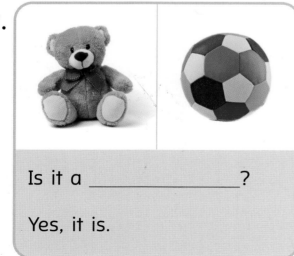

Is it a _____?

Yes, it is.

2.

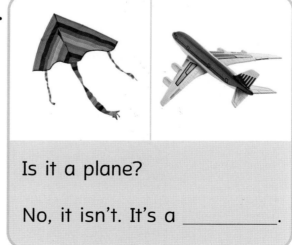

Is it a plane?

No, it isn't. It's a _____.

C Listen and circle. 42))

1. What is the girl's name?

a Hello
Jenny

b Hello
Lucy

c Hello
Amy

2. What is the girl's toy?

a   b   c

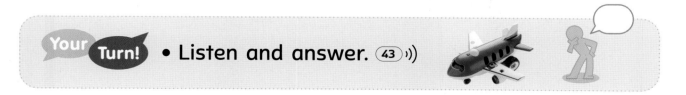

Your **Turn!** • Listen and answer. 43))

A Listen and repeat. 44))

1 bird	2 cat	3 dog
4 hamster	5 rabbit	6 turtle

B Listen and number. 45))

They're dogs.

They're = They are

C Listen and check. 46))

1.

2.

3.

4.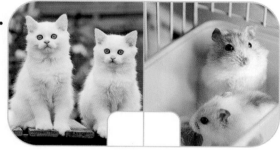

D Listen and match. 47))

1.

2.

3.

What are they?
They're birds.
They're = They are

27

A Listen and number. 48))

B Listen and circle. Then write. 49))

1.

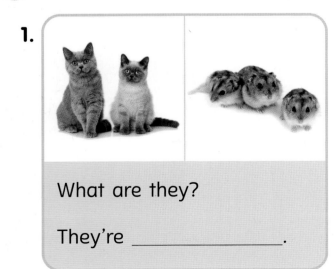

What are they?

They're _____.

2.

What are they?

They're _____.

C Listen and circle. 50))

1. What is the girl's name?

(a)

Hello
Julie

(b)

Hello
Jane

(c)

Hello
Jenna

2. What pet do Joe and Alex want?

(a)

(b)

(c)

Your Turn! • Listen and answer. 51))

A **Listen and draw lines.** 52))

Sam

Kate

Ella

Alex

B **Listen and write.** 53))

1. Whose toy is it?

_____ 's

2. What is in the bag?

_____

C **Listen and check.** 54))

1. Where is Amy?

A ☐

B ☐

2. Who is Amy with?

A ☐

B ☐

A Listen and repeat. 55))

1	2	3	4	5
one	two	three	four	five
6	7	8	9	10
six	seven	eight	nine	ten

B Listen and number. 56))

Six books.

C Listen and check. 57))

1.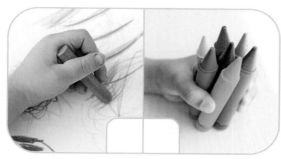

2.

3.

4.

D Listen and color. 58))

1.

2.

3.

How many kites?
Five kites.

A Listen and number. 59))

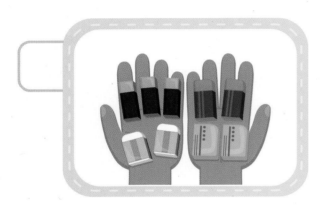

B Listen and circle. Then write. 60))

1.

How many chairs?

_____ chairs.

2.

How many clocks?

_____ clocks.

C Listen and circle. 61))

1. How many planes does Amy have?

ⓐ **6** ⓑ **7** ⓒ **8**

2. What is Ken's toy?

ⓐ  ⓑ  ⓒ

 Your Turn! • Listen and answer. 62))

8 Colors

A Listen and repeat. 63))

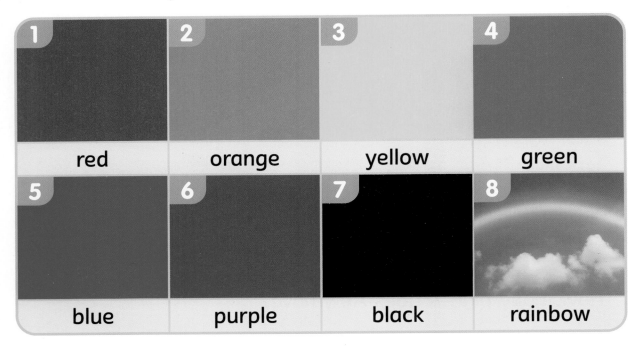

1 red	2 orange	3 yellow	4 green
5 blue	6 purple	7 black	8 rainbow

B Listen and number. 64))

It's red.

It's = It is

C Listen and check. 65))

1.

2.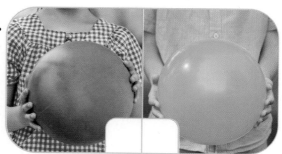

3.

4.

D Listen and number. Then color. 66))

What color is it?
It's yellow.
It's = It is

37

A Listen and number. 67))

B Listen and circle. Then write. 68))

1.

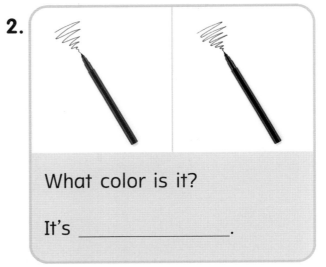

What color is it?

It's _____.

2.

What color is it?

It's _____.

C **Listen and circle.** 69))

1. How many colors are in Bill's rainbow?

ⓐ   ⓑ   ⓒ

2. What is Anna's favorite color?

ⓐ    ⓑ    ⓒ

Your Turn! • **Listen and answer.** 70))

A Listen and repeat. 71))

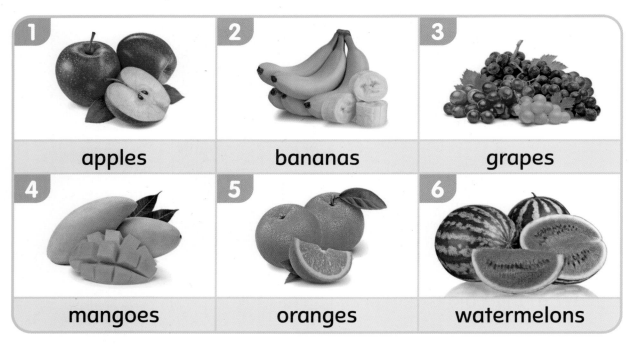

| 1 apples | 2 bananas | 3 grapes |
| mangoes | oranges | watermelons |

B Listen and number. 72))

They're bananas.

They're = They are

C Listen and check. 73))

1.

2.

3.

4.

D Listen and match. 74))

1.  •   •

2.  •   •

3.  •   •

Are they apples?
Yes, they are. / No, they aren't.
aren't = are not

A Listen and number. 75 🔊

B Listen and circle. Then write. 76 🔊

1.

Are they _____?

Yes, they are.

2.

Are they oranges?

No, they aren't.
They're _____.

C Listen and circle. 77))

1. What fruits does Sam see?

ⓐ    ⓑ

2. How many watermelons does Sam's mom get?

ⓐ   ⓑ   ⓒ

Your Turn! • Listen and answer. 78))

A Listen and number. Then write. 79))

[ ]

1   apples

[ ]

[ ]

B Listen and write. 80))

1. What animal is it?

_____

2. What color is it?

_____

C Listen and check. Then color. 81))

• What is in the girl's bag? What colors are they?

☐

☐

☐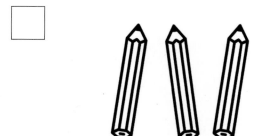

☐

A Listen and repeat. 82))

1 balloon	2 cake	3 candle
4 flower	5 gift	6 table

B Listen and number. 83))

I see a cake.

C Listen and check. 84))

1.

2.

3.

4.

D Listen and match. 85))

1.

2.

3.

What do you see?
I see tables.

A Listen and number. 86 🔊

B Listen and circle. Then write. 87 🔊

1.

What do you see?

I see _____.

2.

What do you see?

I see a _____.

C Listen and circle. 88))

1. How old is Danny?

ⓐ    ⓑ    ⓒ

2. What color is his balloon?

ⓐ    ⓑ    ⓒ

 • Listen and answer. 89))

A Listen and repeat. 90)))

1	**2**	**3**
bears	bees	ducks
4	**5**	**6**
elephants	frogs	lions

B Listen and number. 91)))

Big | Small

Lions are big. Frogs are small.

C Listen and circle. Then check. 92))

1.

  ☐ big   ☑ small

2.

  ☐ big   ☐ small

3.

  ☐ big   ☐ small

4.

  ☐ big   ☐ small

D Listen and circle. 93))

1. bears   (small)

   (frogs)   big

2. ducks   small

   lions   big

3. elephants   small

   bees   big

4. bears   small

   ducks   big

Are frogs big or small?
They're small.
They're = They are

51

A Listen and number. 94))

B Listen and circle. Then write. 95))

1.

Are _____ big or small?

They're small.

2.

Are _____ big or small?

They're big.

C Listen and circle. 96))

1. Where are Ella and Sam?

ⓐ 　　ⓑ 　　ⓒ

2. What big animals do they see?

ⓐ 　　ⓑ 　　ⓒ

Your Turn! • Listen and answer. 97))

A Listen and repeat. 98)))

1 coin	2 marker	3 pen
4 shell	5 watch	6 yo-yo

B Listen and number. 99)))

I have a watch.

C Listen and check. 🔊 100 🔊

1.

2.

3.

4.

D Listen and match. 🔊 101 🔊

1.    •   •

2.    •   •

3.    •   •

What do you have?
I have coins.

A Listen and number. (102)))

B Listen and circle. Then write. (103)))

1.

What do you have?

I have a _____.

2.

What do you have?

I have _____.

C **Listen and circle.** 104))

1. What is in Ben's secret box?

2. What does Jill want?

Your **Turn!**   • **Listen and answer.** 105))

A Listen and draw lines. 106))

Amy

Max

Nina

Ron

B Listen and write. (107)))

1. What does the boy see?

_____

2. Are they big or small?

_____

C Listen and check. (108)))

1. What color is the balloon?

 A ☐    B ☐

2. How many gifts does Ben see?

 A ☐    B ☐

Photo Credits

Shutterstock pp. 6 (OlhaTsiplyar/Max kegfire/Ground Picture), 7 (ESB Professional), 8 (Pixel-Shot/Mtsaride/Alias Studiot Oy/irin-k/Serhiy Stakhnyk), 9 (Bespaliy/tehvon/Natalia Duryagina/Maria Sbytova/MillerTV79/Africa Studio/kana Design Image/Pheelings media), 10 (mik ulyannikov/Andrey Safonov/flyingv3/OlesyaPogosskaya), 11 (Taras Grebinets/New Africa/WachiraS/TuktaBaby/Birgit Reitz-Hofmann/sevenke), 12 (ND700/ziviani/Svetlana MKM/EmBaSy/cosmaa), 13 (New Africa/Svetys12/Africa Studio/SeventyFour/Pixel-Shot/serdiuk yehor/GBJSTOCK/Dmytro Vietrov/Christian Delbert/VALUA/VITALY/Svetlana MKM/Lopolo/sivVector), 18 (stockyimages/grinny/VALUA VITALY/DenisNata/Anatoliy Karlyuk), 19 (fizkes/Dean Drobot/SewCreamStudio/Roman Samborskyi), 20 (DenisProduction.com/pixelheadphoto digitalskillet/Khakimullin Aleksandr/Irina Wilhauk), 21 (wavebreakmedia/Pressmaster/ESB Professional/Ground Picture), 22 (Gerisima/Nadiia Korol/Marco La Melia/SergeyCo/IvanGrabilin/Tanya_mtv), 23 (Juice Flair/smallblackcat/Yurev/Wisut Boonyasopit/FotoDuets/ReaLiia/Krakenimages.com), 25 (IvanGrabilin/Hurst Photo/Ines Behrens-Kunkel/Mouse family), 26 (Adrian Eugen Ciobaniuc/Konstantin Aksenov/Ammit Jack/Johannes Menge/Rita_Kochmarjova), 27 (OCollins/BetterPhoto/Janelle Lugge/Lightspruch/UNIKYLUCKK/Vera Reva/Dora Zett/fantom_rd/Rohit Seth/nicepix/Pixel-Shot/Rosa Jay/Laugesen Mateo/Ermolaev Alexander), 28 (Vlad G/Sinart Creative/Kaewmanee jiangsihui/Kebal Oleksandra/Dora Zett/Ruslan Kudrin/Dan Kosmayer/Rosa Jay), 29 (BearFotos/Svetography/Prachaya Roekdeethaweesab/Nynke van Holten/Oleksandr Lytvynenko), 31 (BestPhotoPlus/Lopolo/miya227/G-Stock Studio), 32 (Zantos), 33 (Gelpi/Patcharida/Ermolaeva Olga 84/The Faces/Boris Bulychev/Mikhailava Alesia/MdMahbuburRahman/KateV28/nix_art), 34 (Passakorn vejchayachai/Sergii_Petruk/gomolach), 35 (InesBazdar/Vadarshop/New Africa/Nadiia Korol/Yellow Cat), 36 (PongMoji), 37 (Chinnapong/Tama2u/Pixel-Shot/Yury Nikolaev/Marko Aliaksandr/Ann in the uk/Uryupina Nadezhda/Natali Brillianata), 38 (Krakenimages.com/Maythaphorn Piyaprichart/bazilpp/Alena Ivochkina), 39(Friends Stock/Vadarshop/photka), 40 Valentyn Volkov/Dmitrij Skorobogatov/Photoongraphy/Maks Narodenko/Tarasyuk Igor), 41 (Denis_Zai/muk woothimanop/PradaBrown/tarapong srichaiyos/Nungning20/PTPO34/S. Soloviev/ABCDstock/Laugesen Mateo/Smart Calendar/Rawpixel.com/JIANG HONGYAN/Anna Nahabed/thodonal88), 43 (FamVeld/Nataly Studio/Boonchuay1970/Photoongraphy/SOMMAI/anusorn2005/MRS.Siwaporn), 44 (Pixel-Shot/Evgeny Karandaev/Africa Studio/nipastock), 46 (TheFarAwayKingdom/Sheila Fitzgerald/Ruth Black/Tiger Images/MG SG/Tohid Hashemkhani), 47 (Africa Studio/allstars/soo hee kim/irina2511/ponsulak/White bear studio/Lifestyle Travel Photo/horiyan/Rawpixel.com/Vladimir Prusakov/Tatyana Vyc/JFunk/Pixel-Shot/New Africa), 48 (AlexSandraSml/Yes I Shoot models/DMITRII SIMAKOV/Fusionstudio/Africa Studio), 49 (Chubykin Arkady/gresei/Susii/GCapture), 50 (PUMPZA/Protasov AN/photomaster/Kletr/Kurit afshen), 51 (stigmatize/Henk Bogaard/Erik Mandre/szefei/Matej Ziak/Maggy Meyer/Mircea Costina/Asaf Weizman), 52 (Sushaaa/Kurit afshen/Ondrej Prosicky/ArtMediaFactory), 53 (photravel_ru/Josef Hanus/karamysh/Daria Rybakova/Alexander Cher/Patryk Kosmider/Eric Isselee), 54 (Tony Baggett/New Africa/Designs Stock/Creatsy/dmytro herasymeniuk/Richard Peterson), 55 (aksenova_sveta/ojellavm/Tetiana Lynnyk/Davaiphotography/ASTroi/Nigita/thananya/BINKONTAN/PicMy/A N D A/Samuel Borges Photography/Mega Pixel/ANURAK PONGPATIMET/tamoncity), 56 (Noey smiley/Kabachki.photo/shi-olga/Viktoriia Pletska2020/AtlasStudio/Olga Popova/BigPixel Photo), 57 (photosync/Olga Popova/Lee Thompson Images), 59 (Susii/gresei/Africa Studio)

C Look and write.

1.
Hello
Amy

_____

2.
Hello
Sam

_____

3.
Hello
Ella

_____

D Listen and write. 02))

1. What's your name?

My name's _____ .

2. What's your name?

My name's _____ .

3. What's your name?

My name's _____ .

3

Dictation Check

A Listen and write. 03))

1.
   Boy 1   Hello. I'm _____. What's your name?

   Boy 2   Hi! My _____'s Alex.

   Boy 1   Nice to meet you.

   Boy 2   Nice to meet you too.

2.
   Boy   Hi. My name's _____. What's your name?

   Girl   Hi. My name's _____.

   Boy   Nice to meet you.

   Girl   Nice to meet you too.

3.
   Girl 1   Hello. I'm _____. What's your name?

   Girl 2   Hi. I'm _____.

   Girl 1   Nice to meet you.

   Girl 2   Nice to meet you too.

Amy   Ben   Ella   Kate   name   Sam

4

Alex   Hello. I'm _____ . What's your _____ ?

Kate   Hi. My name's Kate.

Alex   Nice to _____ you, Kate.

Kate   Nice to meet you too.

Ella   Hi, Alex!

Alex   Oh, hi, Ella! Kate, this is Ella. She's my _____ .

Kate   Hi, _____ . I'm Kate.

Ella   Nice to meet you, Kate.

Kate   Nice to meet you too.

Alex   Let's go play!

Girls   OK.

| Alex | Ella | friend | meet | name |

2 My School Things

Key Word Check

A Look and write.

1.

_____

2.
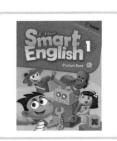

_____

3.

_____

B Listen and write. 05))

1.

What's this?

It's a _____ .

2.

What's this?

It's a _____ .

3.

What's this?

It's a _____ .

C Look and write.

1.

2.

3.

_____ _____ _____

D Listen and write. 06))

1.

What's this?

It's an _____.

2.

What's this?

It's a _____.

3.

What's this?

It's a _____.

7

Dictation Check

A Listen and write. 07))

1.
Boy _____ this?

Girl It's my _____.

Boy I like your ruler.

Girl Thank you.

2.
Girl What's _____?

Boy It's my crayon.

Girl I like your _____.

Boy Thank you.

3.
Boy What's this?

Girl It's _____ book.

Boy I like _____ book.

Girl Thank you.

crayon   my   ruler   this   What's   your

8

Mr. Jones	Hello, Amy.
Amy	Hi, Mr. Jones.
Mr. Jones	Amy, what's this?
Amy	It's my _____.
Mr. Jones	I like your bag. What's in it?
Amy	I'll show you. This is my book.
Mr. Jones	I like your _____.
Amy	Thank you. This is _____ pencil.
Mr. Jones	I like your _____ too.
Amy	Thank you. And this is my _____.
Mr. Jones	Oh, I like it.
Amy	Thank you.

bag   book   my   pencil   ruler

Key Word Check

A Look and write.

1.

2.

3.

_____ _____ _____

B Listen and write. 09))

1.

What is it?

It's a _____ .

2.

What is it?

It's a _____ .

3.

What is it?

It's a _____ .

C Look and write.

1.

2.

3.

_____   _____   _____

D Listen and write. 10)))

1. What is it?

It's a _____ .

2. What is it?

It's a _____ .

3. What is it?

It's a _____ .

A **Listen and write.** 11))

1.

Boy   Hello, Lucy! How are you today?

Girl   I'm good, thank you.

Boy   Hmm. What is _____?

Girl   Wait! I'll show you. Tada! It's a new _____.

Boy   Wow! It's nice!

2.

Girl   Hello, Jake! How are you today?

Boy   I'm good, thank you.

Girl   Hmm. What is it?

Boy   Wait! I'll show you. Tada! It's a new _____.

Girl   Wow! It's _____!

3.

Boy   Hello, Mary! How are you today?

Girl   I'm good, thank you.

Boy   Hmm. _____ is it?

Girl   Wait! I'll show you. Tada! It's a new _____.

Boy   Wow! It's nice!

board   bookcase   chair   it   nice   What

Listen and write. (12) »))

Mr. Jones	Hello, Ella.
Ella	Hi, Mr. Jones.
Mr. Jones	Ella, how are you today?
Ella	I'm good, thank you. Mr. Jones, this is a big _____. What's in it?
Mr. Jones	I'll _____ you.
Ella	OK. What is it? What's in the box?
Mr. Jones	Wait! Tada! It's a _____.
Ella	Wow. It's _____. I like it.
Mr. Jones	I like it too. Oh, Ella, I see something in your bag. What is it?
Ella	Ah! It's a _____.

box   clock   nice   poster   show

My Family

Key Word Check

A **Look and write.**

1.

_____

2.

_____

3.

_____

B **Listen and write.** 13))

1.

Who's he?

He's my _____ .

2.

Who's she?

She's my _____ .

3.

Who's he?

He's my _____ .

C Look and write.

1.

2.

3.

_____   _____   _____

D Listen and write. 14))

1. Who's she?

She's my _____.

2. Who's he?

He's my _____.

3. Who's she?

She's my _____.

Dictation Check

A Listen and write. 15))

1.

Boy   Hey, Emma. Who's she?

Girl   She's my _____.

Boy   She looks _____.

Girl   Thanks, Roy.

2.

Girl   Hey, Tom. Who's he?

Boy   He's my _____.

Girl   He looks _____.

Boy   Thank you, Alice.

3.

Boy   Hi, Jenny. Who's he?

Girl   He's my _____.

Boy   He _____ kind.

Girl   Thank you, Daniel.

brother   grandpa   kind   looks   pretty   sister

16

Listen and write. 16))

Tony	Hi, Ella. What's this?
Ella	Hey, Tony. It's my album.
Tony	Who's she? She _____ kind.
Ella	Thanks. She's my _____. She's very kind. And this is my _____. He's very kind too.
Ella's mom	Hello! Ella, who's your friend?
Ella	Hi, Mom. _____, this is Tony. Tony, this is my mom.
Ella's mom	Hi, Tony. Nice to meet you.
Tony	Nice to _____ you too.
Ella's mom	OK. You guys have fun.

grandma   grandpa   looks   meet   Mom

Key Word Check

A Look and write.

1.

_____

2.

_____

3.

_____

B Listen and write. 17))

1.

Is it a _____ ?

Yes, it is.

2.

Is it a _____ ?

Yes, it is.

3.

Is it a _____ ?

Yes, it is.

C Look and write.

1.

2.

3.

_____   _____   _____ _____

D Listen and write. 18))

1. Is it a ball?

No, it isn't.
It's a _____.

2. Is it a kite?

No, it isn't.
It's a _____.

3. Is it a doll?

No, it isn't.
It's a teddy _____.

A **Listen and write.** 19))

1.
   Boy Hi, Kelly. What's _____?

   Girl Hi, Rob. Guess what this is.

   Boy What is it? Is it a _____?

   Girl Yes, it is!

   Boy Wow! It looks nice!

2.
   Girl Hey, John. What's up?

   Boy Hi, Amy. Guess what this is.

   Girl What is it? Is it a _____?

   Boy No, it _____. It's a robot!

   Girl Wow! It looks nice!

3.
   Boy Hi, Emily. What's up?

   Girl Hey, Ben. _____ what this is.

   Boy What is it? Is it a ball?

   Girl No, it isn't. It's a _____!

   Boy Wow! It looks nice!

doll   Guess   isn't   kite   plane   up

Listen and write. 20))

Jenny   Hi, Alex. What's _____?

Alex   Hi, Jenny. Nothing much. What's this?

Jenny   Take a guess!

Alex   OK. Is it a _____?

Jenny   No, it isn't.

Alex   Umm.... Is it a _____ _____?

Jenny   Nope! It isn't.

Alex   Hmm.... Is it a kite?

Jenny   No, it _____. One last chance!

Alex   Is it a _____?

Jenny   Yes. You're right! It's a ball!

ball	isn't	robot	teddy bear	up

Key Word Check

A **Look and write.**

1.

_____

2.

_____

3.

_____

B **Listen and write.** 21))

1. What are they?

They're _____ .

2. What are they?

They're _____ .

3. What are they?

They're _____ .

C Look and write.

1.

2.

3.

_____   _____   _____

D Listen and write. 22))

1.   What are they?

They're _____.

2.   What are they?

They're _____.

3.   What are they?

They're _____.

Dictation Check

A Listen and write. ㉓)))

1.
   Girl 1 What are they?

   Girl 2 They're _____ .

   Girl 1 I want a _____ !

   Girl 2 Me too!

2.
   Girl What are they?

   Boy They're _____ .

   Girl I want a _____ !

   Boy Me too!

3.
   Boy 1 What are they?

   Boy 2 They're _____ .

   Boy 1 I want a _____ !

   Boy 2 Me too!

dog   dogs   rabbit   rabbits   turtle   turtles

Listen and write. 24))

Joe   Come and look at these!

Julie   What are they? Joe, do you know?

Joe   Julie! They're _____.

Alex   Hi, guys! What's up?

Joe   Hi, Alex. We're looking at _____! Come

and look at these.

Alex   What are they?

Julie   I think they're _____.

Joe   Julie, you're right! They're hamsters.

Alex   I want a _____!

Joe   Me too! Let's go and ask our _____.

cats   hamster   hamsters   moms   pets

Key Word Check

A Look and write.

1. **1**
2. **2**
3. **3**
4. **4**
5. **5**

_____   _____   _____   _____   _____

B Listen and write. 25))

1. How many books?

   _____ book.

2. How many rulers?

   _____ rulers.

3. How many pencils?

   _____ pencils.

 **Look and write.**

1. **6**

2. **7**

3. **8**

4. **9**

5. **10**

_____ _____ _____ _____ _____

D **Listen and write.** 26))

1. How many kites?

   _____ kites.

2. How many kites?

   _____ kites.

3. How many kites?

   _____ kites.

Dictation Check

A Listen and write. 27))

1.

Girl Hi, Alex. Can I borrow your pencils?

Boy _____ many pencils?

Girl _____ pencils.

Boy Sure. Here you go.

2.

Boy Hi, Eva. Can I borrow your erasers?

Girl How _____ erasers?

Boy _____ erasers.

Girl Sure. Here you go.

3.

Girl Hi, Ted. Can I _____ your pens?

Boy How many pens?

Girl _____ pens.

Boy Sure. Here you go.

borrow   Four   How   many   Nine   Three

Listen and write. 28))

Amy   What's up, Ken?

Ken   Hey, Amy. What are they?

Amy   They're my _____.

Ken   You have so _____! How many robots?

Amy   _____ robots.

Ken   How many teddy bears?

Amy   _____ teddy bears.

Ken   How many planes?

Amy   I have _____ planes.

Ken   Wow! I only have _____ toy! It's a ball.

Amy   I have a lot. We can share.

Ken   Thanks. You're the best.

Five   many   one   six   Three   toys

Key Word Check

A Look and write.

1.

2.

3.

4.

_____   _____   _____   _____

B Listen and write. 29))

1.  What color is it?

It's _____.

2. What color is it?

It's _____.

3. What color is it?

It's _____.

C Look and write.

1.

2.

3.

4.

_____   _____   _____   _____

D Listen and write. 30))

1.  What color is it?

It's _____.

2. What color is it?

It's _____.

3. What color is it?

It's _____.

Dictation Check

A **Listen and write.** 31))

1.
   Boy   Come and look at this! It's my new bag!

   Girl   What color is it?

   Boy   It's _____.

   Girl   Orange is my _____ color!

2.
   Girl   Come and look at this! It's my new ball!

   Boy   What color is it?

   Girl   It's _____.

   Boy   Purple is _____ favorite color!

3.
   Boy   Come and look at this! It's my new ruler!

   Girl   What _____ is it?

   Boy   It's _____.

   Girl   Green is my favorite color!

   color   favorite   green   my   orange   purple

Listen and write. 32))

Bill	Anna, look!
Anna	Hey, Bill. What is it?
Bill	It's a _____!
Anna	Well, what _____ is it?
Bill	It's red, orange, _____, green, and blue. It has five colors!
Anna	Bill, I see _____ too! Your rainbow has six colors.
Bill	You're right! Let's mix all the colors together.
Anna	What color is it?
Bill	It's _____. Black is my favorite color! What's your favorite color?
Anna	It's _____! I love the color of the sky!

| black | blue | color | purple | rainbow | yellow |

Key Word Check

A Look and write.

1.

2.

3.

_____   _____   _____

B Listen and write. 33))

1.   Are they _____?

   Yes, they are.

2.   Are they _____?

   Yes, they are.

3.   Are they _____?

   Yes, they are.

C Look and write.

1.

_____

2.

_____

3.

_____

D Listen and write. 34))

1.

Are they apples?

No, they aren't.
They're _____.

2.

Are they bananas?

No, they aren't.
They're _____.

3.

Are they grapes?

No, they aren't.
They're _____.

Dictation Check

Ⓐ Listen and write. 35))

1.

Girl Look what I _____!

Boy Are they _____?

Girl No, they aren't. They're mangoes.

Boy They look yummy.

2.

Boy Look what I have!

Girl Are they watermelons?

Boy No, they aren't. They're _____.

Girl They look _____.

3.

Girl Look what I have!

Boy Are they _____?

Girl Yes, they are.

Boy They _____ yummy.

bananas   grapes   have   look   oranges   yummy

B Listen and write. 36))

Sam	Mom! I see so many _____ !
Mom	Sam, come and look at these.
Sam	What are they? Are they _____ ?
Mom	No, they aren't.
Sam	Hmm. Are they _____ ?
Mom	Yes, they are!
Sam	Mom, what are they?
Mom	They're _____ .
Sam	They look _____ !
Mom	Let's get two, Sam.
Sam	Mom, you're the best!

apples   fruits   mangoes   watermelons   yummy

Key Word Check

A Look and write.

1.

_____

2.

_____

3.

_____

B Listen and write. 37))

1.

What do you see?

I see a _____.

2.

What do you see?

I see _____.

3.

What do you see?

I see _____.

C Look and write.

1.

2.

3.

_____   _____   _____

D Listen and write. 38))

1.   What do you see?

I see _____.

2.   What do you see?

I see _____.

3.   What do you see?

I see _____.

Dictation Check

A **Listen and write.** 39))

1.
   Girl Joe, what do you _____?

   Boy I see _____.

   Girl Do you want one?

   Boy Yes, please!

2.
   Boy Sue, what do you see?

   Girl I see _____.

   Boy Do you _____ one?

   Girl Yes, please!

3.
   Girl Ronnie, what do you see?

   Boy I see _____.

   Girl Do you want one?

   Boy Yes, _____!

balloons   flowers   gifts   please   see   want

B Listen and write. 40))

Aunt Mary	Happy birthday, Danny.
Danny	Thank you, Aunt Mary.
Aunt Mary	Let's get a big birthday _____.
Danny	Yay! Can we get this chocolate cake?
Aunt Mary	Of course. It looks yummy! How _____ are you now, Danny?
Danny	I'm seven years old.
Aunt Mary	OK, you're seven. Let's get seven _____.
Danny	Aunt Mary, look! I see _____.
Aunt Mary	Do you _____ one?
Danny	Yes, _____! Can I get a purple one?
Aunt Mary	Sure.
Danny	Thank you, Aunt Mary. You're the best.

balloons   cake   candles   old   please   want

11 Big or Small

A Look and write.

1.

_____

2.

_____

3.

_____

B Listen and write. 41))

1.

Are _____ big or small?

They're small.

2.

Are _____ big or small?

They're big.

3.

Are _____ big or small?

They're small.

C Look and write.

1.

_____

2.

_____

3.

_____

D Listen and write. 42))

1.

Are _____ big or small?

They're big.

2.

Are _____ big or small?

They're small.

3.

Are _____ big or small?

They're big.

A **Listen and write.** 43))

1.

Boy   Are _____ big or small?

Girl   They're _____.

Boy   How big?

Girl   Really big!

2.

Girl   Are _____ big or small?

Boy   They're _____.

Girl   How small?

Boy   Really small!

3.

Boy   Are _____ big or small?

Girl   They're big.

Boy   How big?

Girl   _____ big!

big   elephants   frogs   lions   Really   small

B Listen and write. 44))

Sam	Here we are, Ella! We're at the _____. Look at all these animals!
Ella	Wow. Sam, I see so many animals! Whoa, look! What are they?
Sam	They're _____.
Ella	Are bears big or small?
Sam	They're _____.
Ella	How big?
Sam	Really big!
Ella	And look! What are they?
Sam	They're ducks.
Ella	Are _____ big or small?
Sam	They're _____.
Ella	How small?
Sam	Really small!
Ella	No, look! This duck is _____ big! Haha!

bears   big   ducks   really   small   zoo

Key Word Check

A Look and write.

1.

_____

2.

_____

3.

_____

B Listen and write. 45))

1.

What do you have?

I have _____.

2.

What do you have?

I have _____.

3.

What do you have?

I have _____.

C Look and write.

1.

2.

3.

_____ _____ _____

D Listen and write. 46))

1. What do you have?

I have _____.

2. What do you have?

I have a _____.

3. What do you have?

I have a _____.

A **Listen and write.** 47))

1.
   Boy   What do you _____?

   Girl   I have _____.

   Boy   Can I have one?

   Girl   Sure. Here you go.

2.
   Girl   What do you have?

   Boy   I have _____.

   Girl   Can I have _____?

   Boy   Sure. Here you go.

3.
   Boy   What do you have?

   Girl   I have _____.

   Boy   Can I have one?

   Girl   Sure. _____ you go.

| coins | have | Here | one | pens | shells |

Ben Hey, Jill. How are you?

Jill   Hi, Ben. I'm good. What's this?

Ben It's my secret _____.

Jill   Well, what do you _____ in it?

Ben I have markers and a _____! They're very

nice.

Jill   Great! How many _____?

Ben Six markers.

Jill   Wow. Can I have a red one?

Ben Sure. Here you go.

Jill   What else do you have in your secret box?

Ben I don't know. It's a _____!

| box | have | markers | secret | yo-yo |

Memo